BODY LOV

28 SPELLBINDING PRACTICES TO BOOST YOUR BODY RELATIONSHIP AND BECOME A BONA FIDE BODY IMAGE WITCH-MERMAID-FAIRY QUEEN

Dri Marie

The Body Joy Academy

Dri Marie/The Body Joy Academy

 Ordering Information:
Quantity sales. Special discounts are available on quantity purchases by corporations, associations, and others. For details, contact the "Special Sales Department" at the address above.

Body Love Magic- 28 spellbinding practices to boost your body relationship and become a bona fide body image witch-mermaid-fairy queen/ Dri Marie —1st ed.
ISBN 978-1-7398156-0-8

TABLE OF CONTENTS

For all the women out there engaged in the sacred and revolutionary work of making peace with their own bodies.

INTRODUCTION

Healing our body relationship is an ever-evolving process of connection.

Dear fabulous witch – mermaid - fairy queen. So, you struggle with your body image. You don't like the way your body looks and you wish she were thinner, or taller, or more muscular, or less bulgy, or more tanned or less freckly, or smoother, with a smaller or bigger chest, thicker or curlier or straighter hair, with "better" proportions, more curves, less curves, fill in the rest.

Body image is a complex thing. It involves nine different areas of our brain, which span our perceptive, affective and cognitive functions. That means that it's hard to study, and that it makes sense that healing our body image should take a little while!

Healing our body relationship is an ever-evolving process of connection. Very much like a relationship with another human being, it takes patience, dedication, education, some compromise, deep listening, a compassionate heart, a willingness to forgive, and all these wisdom-matured ingredients. But we can do that, yes? Yes, we can.

So, dear one, I don't promise that picking up this tiny book will make all your body image woes disappear overnight, although I wish I had a magic wand that could do just that. I guarantee, however, that using some or all of the spellbinding practices contained in this book over the next few months or year will shift n' shake your body relationship for the better.

Because each spell in this book can open a doorway to healing; each practice can unlock a new way of seeing your relationship with your wonderful body; each action step can shake up, dislodge and dispel a toxic belief.

This book contains 28 spellbinding practices, which we will call spells for short. Although I'm a huge fan of Willow from "Buffy The Vampire Slayer", when I say spells, I don't mean wicca-approved spells for which you will need actual ingredients. They will not require you to buy anything pricey or burn anything down. (Though if you have a coven and you want to dance naked around a bonfire of women's mags - be my guest!) These spells are invitations to try something you might not have tried before. That's it.

They are characterised very loosely as yin or yang. This is not scientific or anything - you get the sense by now that this book is a smorgasbord of fun, tiny but big things - but that classification will give you an idea of whether activities are more internal, from the inside-out, longer-term, or reflective practices (yin), or more external, from the outside-in, shorter-term targeted actions (yang.) The spells weave a yin-yang-yin-yang pattern throughout the book.

The way to read this book is with kind curiosity. That's the only rule. Other than that, you can use the book however you wish. You can do what I like to do, which is to use it like an oracle deck: sitting down, breathing deeply, closing your eyes, and opening the book at a random page, trusting that whatever spell you fall on will be the one you need to read today. Or you can work through the spells one by one, from start to finish or finish to start. You can work the yin magic first, and the yang second, or vice versa. You can pick one you like the sound of. It's really up to you and your particular way of working your magic!

Some spells contain writing prompts and points to reflect on. You might want to get yourself a nice journal for those!

May this book be a warm, compassionate, fun-but-wise companion for you, to pick up when you feel the need, to remind you that you're not alone in having body image woes, and that to live in this world wearing a woman's body is sometimes no mean feat.

These spellbinding practices are my take on advice, insights and practices that already live out there in many forms, infused with my own lived experience and that of many women who are, right now, practicing the revolutionary art of learning to love their own body.

The spells in this book are simple, but it doesn't make them (necessarily) easy. Some, like self-compassion and the development of awareness, need to be practiced regularly. You might struggle with some of them and take to others quite naturally. Be your own best friend/good witch/fantabulous land mermaid/fairy godmother as you work through them.

If you're really struggling one day, read the page in the middle of the book, "in case of emergency."

The world needs more body image witches-mermaids-fairy queens to embody body peace, joy and harmony. Ready? Let's work some body love magic together!

P.S: Please note that this book is not a substitute for therapy on body image or other issues. The impact of traumas such as body shaming, body discrimination, body stigma, racism, classism, trans-phobia and living in systemically unequal, patriarchal societies sometimes necessitates seeking help from professionals who are savvy on those various aspects of the embodied experience. Thankfully, many people do that sacred work nowadays, and do it magnificently. Go forth and seek them out, dear one!

Self-compassion is like a muscle: it strengthens with practice.

S elf-compassion is crucial for your body relationship. It's especially essential for bad body image days, when you really struggle.

Follow this sweet kazam when you are in need of deep self-friendship for your body image experience. Feel free to record the steps on your phone and listen back.

Step 1: Sit down somewhere comfy if you can. Put your hand on your heart. Close your eyes. Take a few deep breaths. Feel your feet on the ground and the points of contact your body makes with the surface she is sitting on.

Say to yourself:

So, I am struggling with my body image today. It's tough being embodied. Let me not diss that experience as unworthy or shallow. Feeling uncomfortable in my body, or about my body history, is a painful experience. I am having a hard time with this today.

Step 2: Say to yourself:

We all have bad body image days. I feel very alone in my individual body when I start hating on her. But so many women have those terrible days when their bodies feel like a prison, no matter what they look like.

Visualise yourself standing in a circle with all of the women out there who are struggling, learning and growing, and remember that you are not alone.

Step 3: Say to yourself:

Let me be kind to that part of me that is struggling. What would I say to my best friend if she were experiencing what I am going through? How can I show myself some tenderness? If self-love feels too indulgent, can I settle for simple care, the kind that puts a jacket on my shoulders when I'm cold? What do I need today?

Send yourself kindness, through the hand on your heart.

Open your eyes when you feel complete. And remember, self-compassion is like a muscle: it strengthens with practice.

Weave the spell: sit down to meditate.

SCALE BANISHMENT HEX
Yang

Low stress levels are much more conducive to better health outcomes than a specific number on a scale.

Bin your scale.

Did you just freak out a little?

Let us imagine a world in which what you weigh is not that important and practice being in that world for a bit. Imagine what you might eat, what activities you might pursue, what movement practice you might engage in, what books you might read, what exciting stuff you might buy, if you did not let the number on the scale dictate those choices.

Let us fling open the windows and let in some fresh air into the tiny, dark room we have so far labeled "health". Let us expand our vision of what it really means to be "healthy": physical health is but one component, of which weight is a tiny part. It cannot be emphasised enough that mental and emotional health are of equal and vital importance. In fact, numerous studies have shown that stress and its associated elevated cortisol levels have a huge effect on our overall health- that includes the chronic type of stress related to being the victim of weight stigmatisation, discrimination and shaming.

People who have been shamed for their weight are also more likely to engage in disordered eating, including binge eating and compulsively eating beyond satiety.

In short, equating health with weight is not only dangerously reductive; it can exacerbate problems with food and elevate stress levels! Not good.

Sure, binning your scale can be a little scary. After all, we have *all* been conditioned to equate our weight with our health and to view the pursuit of health as a "super value" (it's called *healthism* and, like many - isms, it ain't pretty). However, a truly holistic approach to health can (and should) look at behaviours, not numbers. Weighing yourself compulsively and letting that number dictate your mood, food choices or movement regardless of your body's actual needs isn't healthy.

I've not weighed myself in years. My clothes do a fine job of letting me know whether I might have put on, or lost, a bit of weight and, more importantly, my stress levels are kept lower by the elimination of compulsive weight checking - and as we now know, low stress levels are much more conducive to better health outcomes than a specific number on a scale.

Weave the spell: bin, sell or smash your scale, or hide it in the attic for at least two months.

Your body relationship can become a solid, and splendid, marriage – able to weather the inevitable storms of life thanks to unflinching commitment and willingness to show up for love.

Remember that body image is a fluctuating thing. It is ever evolving, like a relationship. Even folk with pretty good body relationships are not spared the occasional struggle with their appearance or ability level or age. Being embodied is not an easy thing at times.

One constant is that our bodies will change, be it through ageing, illnesses, loss, pregnancies, miscarriages, menopause, accidents, stress, monthly cycles... or global pandemics.

Those unavoidable things can trigger bad days or bad body image cycles – and that's entirely normal. You don't wake up one day with a "fixed" and shiny body image forever more. That's not how the fairy tale ends. However, your body relationship can become a solid, and splendid, marriage – able to weather the inevitable storms of life thanks to unflinching commitment and willingness to show up for love, through actions small and big and the nurturing of each other.

Bad body image days can also be triggered by more timely life occurrences: looking at old or recent photos, going to a party, facing a reunion of any kind, a breakup, going home to visit family, being in an unfamiliar environment, reading women's magazines, even such things as having just eaten. That's all normal. What we can do is learn resources to roll with life's punches. Recognising that fluctuations in your relationship to your body are entirely normal can help.

Body image is an incredibly complex concept, which involves nine different areas of the brain! Is it any wonder we have no clue what's going on with it sometimes? Let's cut ourselves some slack, in other words, and again, show ourselves compassion.

Weave the spell and journal: What are your body image triggers? What tends to send you for a negative spin? Can you find a mantra to remind you of the Life Cycles Charm?

Examples of mantra: Even though she doesn't look how I think I want her to, I cherish my ever-changing body. May I open to the possibility of loving my changing body. This life will change my body and that is okay. May I accept my ever-changing body just as she is.

FASHIONISTA PHILTRE
Yang

In this day and age, for a woman to feel a little bit fabulous in her body is nothing short of revolutionary.

B uy yourself *one* item of clothing that you love and that fits perfectly. Forget the size label (cut it out if you need to!). Don't be tempted to buy one size down because it sounds better, or because you can't possibly imagine buying a pair of trousers size x, y or z. Your body deserves to be well-clad, comfortable and feeling fantastic.

It took me so long to embrace this principle! We are so conditioned to keep clothes for "when we lose the weight", or to squeeze ourselves into subtly-too-small jeans just to say that we're a size X, that we often balk at the idea of buying something that a) we *love* and that b) fits us now.

This yang philtre works from the outside-in but is a very effective diet culture* takedown. It is empowering in a fun, easy way, but will still require you to make peace, at least for one moment, with whatever size and shape your body is at today.

My friend Rose once said, "I have finally ordered myself a new pair of jeans in a size that actually fits me. It is a size I've never worn before, but the number doesn't matter. I feel comfortable, happy, and a little bit fabulous."

In this day and age, for a woman to feel a little bit fabulous in her body is nothing short of revolutionary! Huzzah for the fashionista!

Weave the spell: go buy that dress, jacket or pair of jeans you've been eyeing up for months.

---

* See glossary at the end of this book.

FAT DAY DRAM
Yin

Cultivating awareness of our changing emotional landscapes can help us to understand our inner life much better and thus enter into a deeper relationship with ourselves.

.

Have you ever had an "I feel fat" day? Those happen regardless of our sizes. There is nothing wrong with being fat - it's time we reclaim that descriptor - but "feeling fat" indicates something other than an objective physical descriptor.

Feeling "fat" is always worth investigating. There's a lot of "fat isn't a feeling" talk in the body image healing sphere, and although that is certainly technically true, I don't find that response particularly helpful, because it dismisses the label that has worked so far for someone to describe a particular set of physical sensations, feelings and thoughts. In itself, the "I feel fat" feeling or statement can be full of nuance, and a doorway to a potentially insightful investigation.

What does "feeling fat" mean for you? I invite you to divide the general "fat sense" into thoughts, emotions and physical sensations. It can be revelatory.

Use your journal to write down your physical sensations during a "fat day" (for example, fullness, restlessness, impulses to move, scream or dance, bloated sensation, heaviness, tension, anything else...)

Write down your thoughts. Is your inner critic having a field day? What is she saying? Notice that this critical voice is not you; it's just a (mean) thought event. (One of my clients calls her inner critic Edwina. Giving the inner critic a name makes it easier to talk her down - "There there, Edwina" - you might want to name yours too!).

Our inner critic loves to make drama, but what is actually happening here and now? Is there really a need to escalate that vague sensation of tightness around the waist? So much that happens in our minds is habit - sometimes completely unhelpful and inaccurate. Awareness is a first step to dismantling what Tara Brach calls "the trance of unworthiness" that can occur, here around the "I feel fat" thing.

Write down your feelings/emotional state. This is where "fat isn't a feeling" is helpful. What are you feeling, really? Sadness? Anger? Disgust? Disappointment? Hopelessness? Tiredness? Longing? (You can find an emotions wheel online to help you home in on your feelings.)

Cultivating awareness of our changing emotional landscapes can help us to understand our inner life much better and thus enter into a deeper relationship with ourselves. In turn, that awareness can help us put our body image experience in perspective.

Weave the spell: journal sensations, feelings and thoughts. What did you learn about the experiential backstage area of your "fat day"?

*See what difference it makes to experience
your body from the inside.*

B ody checking (examining your body in reflective surfaces like mirrors and shop windows, usually to appraise how slim or fat you look) is like weighing yourself with your eyes. It's often compulsive: once we're used to the behaviour, we might not even notice that we're doing it. Building an awareness of how many times a day you check your body for flaws and appraise her size is an important step to boosting your body acceptance.

Once you notice that tendency, practice catching yourself when you do it, and tuning in to how it makes you feel. (Better yet, practice going without (today, for example!) when you sense the impulse.)

See what difference it makes to experience your body from the inside, rather than get lost in the hall of mirrors of a city street or tear yourself to shreds when the image in your bedroom mirror does not fit the "beauty ideal". Yes, it is hard work – keep practicing, dear one. It's worth it to get your life back.

Weave the spell: keep track of your body checking habit today. Connect back to your senses as you look away from your reflection.

Ask yourself: what do you want your body to know at this time? Listen deep, She might write back.

Carve out an hour (or twice 30 minutes during which you will be undisturbed) to write a letter to your body. It might be that you want to honour the grief that comes from not having the body that you wish you had. It might be that you want to show her gratitude. It might be that you need to forgive her, or yourself, or that you simply want to connect with her.

Ask yourself: What do you want your body to know at this time? What do you need to say to her? Address her as you would a person, a She, not an It. You can set a timer to 15 minutes and just free flow - pen never leaving the page. Then take a few deep breaths, go have a cuppa, and come back to your notebook.

Listen deep, She might write back... get ready to write her answers down, again, for 15 minutes. What does she need? What does she wish you knew about her? What's the next step in your collective healing? Have blankets, cups of tea and tissues at the ready, as this enchantment can go deep.

Weave the spell: find a cozy space, get quiet and get writing!

What delights your senses?

Pamper your body! Sometimes nothing says "I care" like a bubble bath with a colourful Lush - or any other preferred pamper retailer - bath bomb! I stand convinced that pampering is not just skin deep. Self-care through engagement in a sensory, sensual activity (warm water, lovely scents, candlelight, etc) just for you and your body is an important gateway to strong body image.

What scents, colours, fabrics and textures do you love? What delights your senses? When I feel a bit worn out and body-weary, the extra post-shower step of putting on a nice body lotion can give me an instant boost. Forget about doing it to "have nice skin glow" or "get rid of wrinkles". Do it because it smells nice, because it's sensual, because it engages your senses.

It doesn't have to come at a high price either. Please don't max out your credit card on extravagant French moisturisers unless you really, really want to! Adding a few drops of essential oil to the bath, buying a small jar of hand lotion or a nicely scented lip balm are all examples of small pampering gestures you can offer your body.

Weave the spell: show your body some love with a sensual delight that suits your tastes and budget!

What does your body love?

I adore the Mary Oliver poem "Wild Geese", and its magical line: "You only have to let the soft animal of your body love what it loves."

What does your body love? From curling up with a book and a cuppa to going hill walking, from playing with kids to wild swimming, make a list and add to it once in a while. Aim to bring those things into your life more often. Keep the list visible and remind yourself of how good it feels to be IN your body as opposed to looking AT it from the outside.

Weave the spell: write a list of what your body loves. Do one of those things this week.

PACHAMAMA TONIC
Yang

Our bodies are stardust.

Pachamama is the ancient Quechua word for
Mother Earth. A wonderful elixir for body
image woes is getting into nature. Our bodies
are stardust. Our bodies are intimately connected to,
and made up of, the same star stuff as trees, as water.
There is nothing like a walk in the forest, or along a
river, up a mountain, or barefoot upon a shore to
place your body within the perspective of the bigger
body of the world.

Can you tempt yourself to get into the water? Have a
sea swim or a paddle in a stream? I love that
particular Pachamama gift, but it is one that we can
easily refuse ourselves if we feel our bodies won't
look good in a swimsuit. The good news is that there

are more and more supportive women's swimming circles out there. If you have mermaid blood, check them out!

Let Pachamama, Mother Earth, hold your body in her bosom – reach down and enfold her sacred earth in your hands, lose yourself in her endless skies, inhale the rich scent of her pine trees, immerse yourself in her cleansing waters, listen to the music of your footsteps on her soft forest floor and to the ancient rhythm of her ocean waves. Feast your senses and take your place in, as Mary Oliver says, "the family of things".

Weave the spell: seek out the natural environment this week if you can and immerse yourself in it.

MINDFUL*MEDICINE
Yin

I send gratitude to my whole body for all she does.

Take yourself through a body gratitude meditation. (I recorded one at https://insighttimer.com/drimarie/guided-meditations/body-gratitude-for-women, but feel free to record this script on your phone to take yourself through it.)

Let your eyes close gently if that feels okay for you.

Take a few deep breaths to help yourself arrive in your body today. Take a deep breath in, filling the lungs, and feel the

---

* See glossary at the end of this book.

expansion in the body... A long, slow exhale, releasing tension in the face and around the eyes. Softening, softening... Deep inhale, filling the belly, feeling the chest and the ribcage expand. Long, slow exhale, letting go of tension in the neck and the shoulders, arms, hands... A deep inhale... Again, feeling that expansion, all the sensations of taking that breath in, holding at the top, just for a bit... Living that fullness... And a long, slow exhale, letting go of any remaining tension and letting that exhale just bring you in your body.

Place your hand gently on your heart and invite in a sense of gratitude... This can be done by simply thinking of something you are feeling grateful for now... even something as simple as having a roof over your head, having time to do this meditation... Sensing what gratitude feels like in your heart.

Maybe if there is a colour to that feeling, imagine that colour filling your heart and gradually expanding to fill your whole body and even a bit beyond, like a cocoon.

Now the invitation is to let the following words and phrases seep into your body, to seep into that cocoon that we've created.

I'm grateful to my body for taking me through my days, taking me through life... for all the things that she does for me daily.

I'm grateful to my feet, helping me ground myself on the earth... Helping me feel my roots and walk through my days. Sending that light touch of gratitude to your feet.

I'm grateful for my legs, the long strong muscles of the thighs, the calves... helping me to walk, to run, swim, to dance, to move in the ways I love; for carrying me through my days... Sensing that gratitude for your legs, all the work that they do.

I am grateful to my bottom helping me cushion my seat, helping me to sit down when I need to rest. I send gratitude to my bottom.

I am grateful to my hips, helping me bend, swivel, allowing me to dance... Sending that colour, that warmth of gratitude around your hips and the pelvic area.

I'm grateful to my belly for helping me digest food and experiences, helping me process what needs to be let go of, what needs to be taken in, keeping me nourished and well fed. Sending gratitude to my belly...

I am grateful to my chest, the house and home of my heart, my lungs. Helping me take in and release breath... Helping keep my precious organs protected. Sending gratitude all around my chest...

I am grateful to my shoulders for carrying so much, so much of life... Sending gratitude to my strong shoulders, and all the way down my arms and my hands that allow me to embrace the people I love, to apprehend the world in a sensual way through my touch, my hands crafting, writing, so grateful to my arms and hands...

Sending gratitude and thanks to my back, my spine, keeping me upright, standing tall, keeping my skeleton in balance... I thank the muscles of the back. Sending gratitude to my whole back.

I'm grateful to my neck and my throat, the seat of my expression and voice, keeping my head up, freeing the flow of energy and being... so much gratitude to my neck and throat.

I'm so grateful to my face for allowing me to express myself in the world. For the people I love to recognize me through my face... my mouth for tasting delicious food, my nose for smelling wonderful fragrances... My eyes, to gaze on the people I love, my ears for listening to music, to voices, to meditations...

I am grateful to my mind, my brain. Keeping this whole operation going, helping me to form thoughts and ideas... To understand, comprehend, grow, learn and share.

Sending gratitude to my whole body for all that she does, breathing in once more that colour and energy, that warmth of gratitude.

Bring your hand back to your heart if it has left it and really feel the warmth there. This is simple, gentle care. Giving thanks to your body for all that she is, all that she was and all that she will be.

Feel free to rest here for as long as you wish. If you're ready to come out of the meditation, find some movement in your fingers and your toes... Give yourself a nice big stretch and open your eyes when you're ready.

Weave the spell: sit or lie down and meditate.

INSTA INCANTATION
Yang

Who do you really wanna hang out with?

I t's time to detox your social media feed. Go through your Insta, Facebook, Twitter – whichever platform you use most regularly – and delete/unfollow any account that makes you feel shit about your body and/or eating and exercise habits.

The young, white, slim yogini who bends herself into pretzels while going on about her green juice cleanses; the fashionable influencer who pollutes your feed with endless filtered selfies; the self-proclaimed nutrition guru who worships at the altar of expensive supplements that you can't pronounce; even the friend who's gone paleo and whose feed has become one giant diet ad. (Note that it's okay if you are dieting and actively part of that community– we have a right to do as we wish with our bodies– but notice whether or not communities that revolve around a restrictive food message will be friends to your body image in the long run.)

Who do you really wanna hang out with? If looking at your feed for a couple of minutes gets you down on yourself, your wonderful body, or your love of cupcakes, unfollow with reckless abandon! Find the #antidiet, #bodyjustice*, #fatpositive and #bodyliberation communities out there. They exist, and they are fabulous.

Weave the spell: choose one of your social media accounts and make it body supportive.

---

* See glossary at the end of this book.

FEMINIST BREW
Yin

You do not have to engage in talk about shrinking women and denying our hunger(s).

Realise your feminism by walking out of diet talk, which is an insidious form of negative bonding and normative discontent - women talking trash about what they eat and what they look like.

How many times have you sat in on diet chats among women? From the colleague who passes moral judgements on the contents of your Tupperware, to the one who can't have cake because her "syns" are already accounted for; from the one who can't wait to tell you about her recent weight loss, to the one who proselytises about her new restrictive keto regimen - diet talk is ubiquitous, and subtly (or not) keeps body dissatisfaction and judgements on food choices and body size bubbling away unchecked.

I will say again that if you are on a diet as you read these words, you have a right to be, and you might even feel like you don't have a choice. I'm here to tell you otherwise, that you can choose to care for and cherish your body regardless of her size. In my opinion, and that of increasing bodies of research, dieting will not help, and almost certainly harm, your body image, in addition to doing untold damage to your metabolism and psychology.

The demonising of certain food groups and body shapes is called diet culture* and is ubiquitous in Western cultures, but you don't actually have to consent to it.

You can up and leave, if that's available. If you're feeling brave, you can calmly state that you are healing your relationship with your body and that you won't engage in diet talk. You can stay quiet, smile and change the subject. You can counter the talk with praise of your new intuitive eating* practice.

The options vary depending on how feisty you feel, but the point is: you do not have to engage anymore, ever, in talk about shrinking women and denying our hunger(s). Ever.

---

* See glossary at the end of this book.

Weave the spell: notice diet talk and value judgements on food. Read up on intuitive eating and diet culture. Respond accordingly.

Surround yourself with women who are actively working on healing their body relationship.

Thank Goddess there are so many fantastic books out there about anti-diet approaches and body positivity*! A life-affirming step for any body -love -magic bibliophile is to start gathering the goods. Look for anti-diet, health at every size*, body respect, body justice*, body positivity, weight-neutral, intuitive eating*, and body image healing resources. There is a non-exhaustive list at the end of this book to get you started.

---

* See glossary at the end of this book.

Stay away from anything that mentions weight loss as a goal - it is of NO help to anyone struggling with disordered eating or body image issues. Some folk out there are peddling intuitive eating as a weight-loss tool (RUN! RUN LIKE HELL!), and often the mindful eating selections carry fat phobic, weight-loss-oriented messages (much to my despair, as I am a big fan of mindfulness practices for body connection.)

Connect with nourishing sources, and with body freedom circles, on or offline. Surround yourself with women who are actively working on healing their body relationship, or already are role models for body justice. Thankfully there seems to be more of us out there than ever before!

Weave the spell: have a look at the list of resources at the end of this book. Choose one that appeals to you and start exploring!

IN CASE OF EMERGENCY

STEP AWAY FROM THE MIRROR. SIT DOWN IF YOU CAN.

FEEL YOUR FEET ON THE GROUND. SENSE THE EARTH CARRYING YOU.

WHAT CAN YOU SEE AROUND YOU – AWAY FROM YOUR REFLECTION?

CLOSE YOUR EYES IF THAT FEELS COMFORTABLE FOR YOU. IF NOT, LOWER OR SOFTEN YOUR GAZE.

WHAT CAN YOU TOUCH?
WHAT CAN YOU SMELL?
WHAT CAN YOU TASTE?
WHAT CAN YOU HEAR?

IF THAT FEELS COMFORTABLE FOR YOU, RELAX INTO YOUR BREATH. FEEL THE SENSATIONS THAT THE WAVES OF BREATH

CREATE IN YOUR BODY.

LET YOUR BREATH BE YOUR FRIEND.
IF STAYING WITH THE BREATH IS
DIFFICULT, BRING YOUR AWARENESS INTO
YOUR HANDS AND FEET. SENSE WHERE
THEY REST, FEEL INTO THEIR WARMTH.

SAY TO YOURSELF: I AM HERE. IN THIS
BREATH, I AM OK. (OR, IN THIS WARMTH, I
AM OK.)

PUT A HAND ON YOUR HEART. FEEL ITS
KIND TOUCH.

SAY TO YOURSELF: MAY I ACCEPT MYSELF
JUST AS I AM.

STAY AS LONG AS YOU NEED.

REPEAT AS NECESSARY.

Identify and rectify when you self-objectify.

Women are conditioned from an early (and getting earlier) age to self-objectify. Sometimes as early as six years old, girls realise that they get praised or appraised on their looks and that their appearance seems to matter more than that of boys. (For example, my niece was four when she first asked me about beauty and whether it was important, whether she (or I) was beautiful, but my nephews never have.)

This jinx warrants an entire book and excellent ones have already been written on the subject (Please make "More Than A Body", by the Kite sisters, part of your body freedom library). Please, my dear, make this objection to self-objectification yours by all the means available to you.

We are not decorations, and it should revolt us all that we should be treated as such, even when we're the ones doing it!

Weave the spell: identify and rectify when you self-objectify! A useful mantra can be: my body is a She, not an It; I choose to focus on what She can do.

Intuitive eating is about reconnection with our hunger(s), finding joy in movement, and delight in our bodies just as they are now.

D iet culture* is a system of beliefs that demonises certain foods and body types while elevating others. It tells women (especially) that their bodies are a problem, in order to sell them the solution. It is the source of the majority of our disordered eating behaviours and body image issues. And nothing says "f*** you, diet culture" like embracing intuitive eating*.

---

* See glossary at the end of this book.

Intuitive eating is about reconnection with our hunger(s), finding joy in movement, and delight in our bodies just as they are now. It is about trusting the wisdom of our bodies, engaging in holistic self-care and not being taken in by the latest "wellness gurus". It is about empowering ourselves and not spending our resources on trying to shrink ourselves forever more. It's about health on our own terms, body justice, addressing systemic inequalities in healthcare settings and calling out weight stigmatisation*.

It's about learning to be with our feelings, asserting what we need, and standing up for our Goddess-given right to nourishment without judgement whatever our shape or size.

Diet culture hates that stuff.

Thankfully, intuitive eating is becoming more and more recognised as a valuable and health-promoting practice. Dietitians, fitness professionals and healthcare providers are starting to engage with it and the Health at Every Size®* movement. So whether it's with The Body Joy Academy or another anti-diet practitioner, if you really really really wanna zig-a-zig and ditch diet culture for good, start your intuitive eating practice today. You will never look back.

---

* See glossary at the end of this book.

Weave the spell: to start your intuitive eating practice, find some resources you love and dive in. For articles and resources, visit www.thebodyjoyacademy.com or check out the handy list at the end of this book.

LOVE LETTER LIBATION
Yin

Shower your body with compliments.

Take out a notebook and pen and list all the things you appreciate/like/love about your body. Try and get as many things down as you can. No matter how small. Put self-consciousness aside and shower your body with compliments. Let her drink this sah-weet libation. Nobody needs to know, and She deserves it.

Weave the spell: get quiet and cozy, and go for it.

It's time to get critical about the way size is portrayed in popular culture.

What are your favourite movies or TV series? Who are the characters in them? Is anyone in a larger body? What is their story? How are they portrayed? Are they graced with a complex, interesting personality or reduced to a cliché? Are they allowed normal romance or is it something they need to earn (by losing weight) or forever be denied? Or is their weight constantly mentioned as a "thing"?

It's time to get critical about the way size is portrayed in popular culture.

(A few examples that come to my mind: Evan's larger-bodied sister in "*Atypical*" is a seemingly none-too-bright baker; Sadness in "*Inside Out*" – an otherwise fab film – is plump, while Joy is slim; "fat Monica" in "*Friends*" acquires a completely different personality from her thin self – at once bubblier and less clever; that poor Portuguese lass from "*Love Actually*" is brought out to Colin Firth's character and publicly fat shamed for comedic value. And poor Barb in "*Stranger Things*" not only doesn't get any romance, but gets swiftly disposed of after a couple of episodes. The list goes on!)

All too often, people in larger bodies are portrayed as obsessed with food or big eaters, as less clever than their thin counterparts, as sad or depressed, and certainly as unworthy of a romantic storyline.

Our collective discourse around people in larger bodies shape our mentalities and, more often than not, support the diet culture narrative of "thinner is better", especially for women. Please note this doesn't mean you have to stop watching the shows you love! But getting savvy around the stories we let in means we can start standing up to them and offering alternatives.

Weave the spell: take out your journal and reflect on what you notice about the portrayal of characters in larger bodies in your favourite shows and films or magazines and commercials.
Check out body positive shows on TV and film: Hulu's "Shrill", Netflix's "Dumpling", Percy Adlon's "Bagdad Café", Olivia Wilde's "Booksmart" … Feel free to email the author if you know great examples!

How can I best support my body through the external and internal seasons?

You might have heard about cycle syncing* , following the lunar calendar or the Wheel of the Year in pagan traditions.

Learning about the external cycles of seasons, moon phases and the internal monthly cycle can be a lovely way to become more intimate with your body and what she needs at different times of the week/month/year.

---

* See glossary at the end of this book.

By and large, we aren't taught the wisdom of connecting to our nature and body cycles. That lack causes us to push when we need to rest, close down when we need to open up, and generally deny ourselves the nourishment we would deeply benefit from at specific times of the cycle(s).

Wherever you are as you read this, ask yourself: what is the external season? What point am I at in my cycle? (Winter is your period, if you are still menstruating) What season of life am I in? What qualities of those phases can I absorb or reflect on? How can I support my body best through these?

When we observe the seasons externally and internally, we allow ourselves to open up to the idea of change. We realise that letting go and grieving are experiences as essential as welcoming in and celebrating.

Weave the spell: keep yin and reflect on the season you are in, or make the spell more yang and seek out cycle sync courses, seasonal pagan celebrations and recipe books, women's circles that focus on cycles, or buy yourself a moon calendar or diary (I love the We'Moon diaries, for example.)

Become your own best friend and biggest cheerleader, nurturing mama and fierce protector.

Whatever your views on medicine in general, looking after your human instrument is a good doorway for strengthening your body relationship. Are you getting regular medical check-ups? Are you getting enough rest? Do you have adaptive stress management resources - a meditation practice, a hobby you love, a strong sense of boundaries, movement you enjoy taking part in? (See Spell #26, Movement Magick, for some thoughts on joyful moving!)

A lot of us don't rest enough, have poor time or energy boundaries, or engage in on-again/off-again disordered relationships with exercise. A lot of us spend waaaaaaaaaaaaaaaaaaaaaaaayyyyyyyyyyyyyyyyyy too much time on our phones and social media. A lot of us engage in maladaptive stress management, like drinking or working too much, or numbing out with food regularly.

Thankfully, many resources exist out there that teach us how to swim against the mainstream of overstimulation, exhaustion and disconnection, some of which I listed at the end of this book.

Learn to rest. Book a retreat. Meditate. Move. Leave your phone at home. Unplug for a bit. Stroke the cat, pet the dog, play hide and seek with your kiddos, nephews or nieces, put boundaries around your time, stay away from crazy-makers, learn to say no without guilt. Get that health check. Book that massage, that new course, that hobby.

Become your own best friend and biggest cheerleader, nurturing mama and fierce protector. That, my friend, is self-care caballistica. (Oh, and make up words. It's fun, and it's free!)

Weave the spell: take out your journal and reflect. What do you require to blossom and flourish? What is essential to your wellbeing? You can imagine yourself as a human plant- beyond water and sunlight, what does the "You" plant need?

What qualities can you celebrate in yourself?

When I last saw my two adorable nieces, they decided we should write a story about mermaids. First, my eldest niece started listing what the different mermaids wore and the colour of their hair and eyes. After a little bit of imagination at that level, I introduced her to the concept of personalities and qualities that define a character too. Both nieces really got into that game and soon all our mermaids were brave, funny, intelligent and kind. (There'll be more time to introduce contrast and conflict into their storytelling, I'm sure!)

What do the people who love you see when they look at you? I bet they're not too concerned about the way you look, although they probably think you're gorgeous - they love you after all! But my guess is, they appreciate you way beyond your looks; for the qualities that you emanate, your presence, kindness, intelligence, humour, courage, joy, insight, wisdom, playfulness, creativity, fun, adventurousness, heart...

Imagine now that you are your own best friend (or imagine your actual bestie). What qualities can you celebrate in yourself? What are your strengths and endearing traits? Journal it. No one needs to read it. Toot your own horn shamelessly. Recognise your awesomeness, if only for just this time, although I encourage you to remind yourself of it often. This is not about wishful thinking: seriously ask yourself what your best friend - who adores you - celebrates about you. Therein lies your worth and your innate goodness.

In Percy Adlon's wonderful film "*Bagdad Café*" *, a drama-addicted woman one day leaves the once dingy, conflict-filled motel that has suddenly become full of joy through the chance arrival of the main character. When asked why she is leaving, the drama addict replies: "Too much harmony". The more you fill your inner space with genuine kindness, the less room you make for the drama-addicted inner critic.

* A rare example of a story in which the main character is fat, complex, and loved for who she is.

Weave the spell: get quiet and cozy and write out your worth.

Is there a body part you can appreciate for its delightful functionality?

A s you go about your day, set reminders on your phone or laptop or analogue clock (I'm sure that can work!) throughout the day for a minute to appreciate what your body does for you.

Did you go for a walk today? Send your legs some appreciation.

Did you sit at your desk typing? Your arms, hands and eyes deserve kudos.

Your hips and knees engage in bending and turning; your neck and shoulders carry the weight of your head; your feet help you make contact with the earth; your arms can embrace a loved human or pet.

Whatever your level of ability, is there a body part, organ, limb that you can appreciate for its delightful functionality? Your body is made up of 37.2 trillion cells, each much more complex than the entire city of New York, and all working together in unison ... you, my dear, are a marvel! The idea here is to take the focus, once again, away from experiencing your body as decorative and to delight in all the instrumental goodness that she offers you.

Weave the spell: set a reminder for three moments today to take a breath and send your body some appreciation.

The bedrock of a strong body relationship is made up of many things, such as a sense of purpose and alignment with your innermost values.

When we spend too much time on the outside of our body looking in, we can sometimes lose track of the deeper things. The bedrock of a strong body relationship is not a perfect-looking body. It is made up of many things such as community belonging, a sense of safety in the world, and a sense of purpose and alignment with your innermost values.

Although community belonging and a sense of safety can be compromised by experiences of discrimination – if you live in a larger body for example, or if you regularly experience racism, or belong to any underprivileged group – a sense of purpose and values is yours and yours alone to develop and get intimate with.

Dear one, what are your values? A quick Internet search will bring up many lists of values. Print one out and pick your top 30. Look at your list and see if you can weed out the ones that concern external factors, such as appearance, to hone in on internal values until you have 20 words left.

Are some of them related? Roughly divide the 20 into 5 different categories. In each of those five, which value stands out the most and gives you that sense of something clicking into place? Which value seems to sum up the other words and could be picked as the title for that category? Those are your 5 core values. (For example, my values are creativity, spirituality, growth, community and kindness.)

Do you feel that your life aligns with them right now? Are you living from them, or actively working towards their development? No judgement, remember! Kind curiosity is the attitude we need.

Now that you have your values, your sense of purpose might become a bit clearer if it isn't already. Take clues as well from the things you loved to do as a child, the things you are naturally good at, the things that you enjoy. And remember that actively searching for your life's purpose is a purpose in itself.

Weave the spell: find a list of values online and start homing in on yours.

ARTIST ALLURE
Yang

You, my dear, are a work of art.

Y ou, my dear, are a work of art. A true artist is not so much concerned with a fixed idea of beauty as she is with truth, vitality, spark, colour, character, the way the light falls around people and things, and the shapes that bodies, faces, objects and natural things make.

Try this exercise one day when you can be undisturbed for ten minutes.

Stand in front of the mirror - start with standing in clothes if you have never done this before - and describe yourself out loud in the most objective way possible, as if you were giving directions to a tender, compassionate painter who couldn't see you. They do not want to hear self-judgement - they aren't interested in that. They want to hear about your shape, colours, light and shadows, and proportions of one thing to another.

So instead of saying that "this woman's got terrible thighs and an ugly nose" (what's a painter supposed to do with that? What do these things mean anyway?), say: "her thighs are a round shape, with lightly dimpled, pink-toned white skin, they are about the same length as that of the full arms; her nose is narrow at the top and a bit wider at the bottom with oval nostrils..."

Now the artist's got something to work with - and they'll probably infuse your portrait with the essence of your voice, too.

If you're feeling brave, you can do this standing in your underwear. If you're feeling especially courageous, feel free to practice naked!

Weave the spell: experience yourself as the work of art you are. Practice looking at yourself as if through an artist's lens. If you're feeling bold, imagine you are one particular artist's muse!

WILD WRITING WITCHERY
Yin

Tell your body story.

Wild writing is timed, free-flow, pen-not-leaving-the-page writing. It doesn't preoccupy itself with being good. It's just about showing up on the page, warts and all. And it can do wonders for exploring your body relationship. Here's how it works:

Find a place where you'll be undisturbed for 15, 20 or 25 minutes.

Grab a notebook and pen.

Choose from the following prompts, or devise your own. Your prompt will be your anchor in the mad flow of writing - when your thoughts dry up and you find yourself wondering what to write, go back to your prompt. It doesn't matter if you write it several times in a row until you catch another train of thought.

My body is...

I thank my body for...

Let me tell you my body story.

As a child, my body and I were...

As a teenager, my body and I were...

In my (insert decade), my body and I were...

What I don't want you to know about my body is...

My body wants to tell me things.

Set a timer for your desired length of time. Starting with your prompt, write for that time, pen never leaving the page. Let it all hang out. No one will see what you write unless you want them to. It doesn't have to be anything "good". Let go into the flow.

When the timer rings, feel free to stop or go on. Be gentle after the session – have a cuppa, take a deep breath, let things stir inside of you. Repeat if and when you wish.

Weave the spell: get quiet and cozy and start writing!

MOVEMENT MAGICK
Yang

*We need to snatch joyful movement from the
jaws of punishing exercise.*

One of the best, most glorious, and most fun
ways of reconnecting with our bodies from the
inside is to get them moving. Nothing else
gives us quite the same sense of being **in** our bodies.
We were made to move, and we need to snatch joyful
movement from the jaws of punishing exercise.

First, separate movement from weight loss or a
particular aesthetic goal. Nothing can make
movement seem unpalatable like an elusive ideal
weight/body shape to attain. Inevitably, either the
goal posts move if we do reach them, or we never
reach them in the first place, so we give up on
movement altogether.

How do you love to move? If attaining a particular look or weight weren't part of the equation, what would you choose to do? Dance? Swim? Take up a martial art? Walk? Hill walk? Climb? Horse ride? Play team sports? Tennis? Golf? Lift weights? Attend fun workouts? Yoga? Spin? Zumba? Run? Take up archery? Swing dance? Rollerblading? How can you start bringing that activity into your life?

What does your body enjoy? What kind of movement would you do anyway because you love it?

Sweaty exercise is totally fine if that is truly what makes your body happy. But not all movement need be sweaty, or hard. Once you reconnect to moving your bod for the sheer joy and fun of it, regardless of results, you'll see that you have much more enthusiasm for it than you ever thought possible. I dare you to make movement fun. Therein lies the magick.

Weave the spell: choose a joyful way to move your body this week. How does it make you feel? What is it like to be in your body when she moves?

SPIRITS OF SPIRIT
Yin

Can you connect to the idea that you, your being and your body, are sacred?

This one is especially for you if you believe in a higher power of any kind. God, Goddess, the Universe, Pachamama, a benevolent force, Love...

Can you connect to the idea that you, your being and body, are sacred? Made in the way that you are for a reason? Perhaps being embodied in this particular you-shape is exactly what the Divine intended for your lifetime. Perhaps the lessons that you learn through this particular body - whatever her shape, size, ethnicity, ability, gender identity - are holy lessons for this life of yours. It is clear that our experience of the world will differ according to the kind of human body we are born in/with.

For some of us, experiencing ourselves as connected to divinity/higher power/source/love is a doorway into body reconciliation and acceptance.

To go further, it becomes easier to experience your body as an instrument of love and vessel for radiant inner qualities when you feel connected to a holy source.

Weave the spell: if you are a spiritual or religious person, make sure to include your own body in your prayers, gratitude practices and meditations.

HERSTORICAL HOCUS-POCUS
Yang

Stand against beauty tyranny and declare that your worth might just lie beyond what you look like.

Time to do a little research, dear body image witch-mermaid-fairy queen!

If you find yourself getting stuck on the beauty standards of the day, and realise that your internalised ideal is very narrow, take a path down memory lane of past beauty ideals. Dig up images of Neolithic goddesses, with their voluptuous thighs, bellies and breasts. Feast your eyes on the curvy figures of Renaissance Venuses. See how even during the course of the 20th century, a few decades sufficed for the beauty ideal to go from the very voluptuous Lillian Russell to the teeny tiny Twiggy.

Broadening your beauty horizons will help you realise that beauty standards are ephemeral and, ultimately, only mean what we make them mean: we don't need to give them half as much power as we usually do. What's "in" today will be "out" tomorrow, and ideas of beauty change from culture to culture anyway. One culture's beautiful is not necessarily another's. Can we continue to attach so much importance to those fickle fancies?

It's our job as body image revolutionaries to recognise how often female beauty ideals are steeped in classism (the size of the woman, whatever it may be, indicating the status of the husband), racism (skin lightening and the terrifying concept of "mejorar la raza" in Latin American countries, indicating that one should have children with a white person to make them better-looking) and patriarchal power.

Isn't it much better then to stand against beauty tyranny and declare that our worth might just lie beyond what we look like? Let's start writing a better herstory.

Weave the spell: create a vision board of amazing women that are celebrated through history for their vision, activism, intelligence, wit, or kindness.

GLOSSARY OF TERMS

BODY JUSTICE: A movement that encompasses body positivity, body neutrality, fat acceptance and social justice.

BODY POSITIVITY: A movement focused on the acceptance of all bodies, regardless of size, shape, skin tone, gender, and physical abilities, while challenging present-day beauty standards as an undesirable social construct. Some argue that body positivity has been co-opted by diet culture, and indeed representatives of the movement on social media platforms are largely young, white, slim, toned and able-bodied, so although body positivity is a good thing, it's worth asking questions if body diversity isn't in evidence.

CYCLE SYNCING: The art and practice of syncing the different phases of the menstrual cycle to the type of physical, mental and social activities we engage in, respecting the energy of the various phases.

DIET CULTURE: A set of beliefs that values thinness, appearance and shape over health and wellbeing, or sometimes equates health with weight. It demonises certain foods and body shapes while exalting others. Its offspring are, among others, body shaming of self or others, restriction in eating, and weight or food obsessions.

WEIGHT STIGMA: Weight stigma refers to the discriminatory acts and ideologies targeted towards individuals because of their weight and size. Weight stigma is a result of weight bias. Weight bias refers to the negative ideologies associated with larger bodies.

HEALTH AT EVERY SIZE®: Health at Every Size® is an approach to public health that seeks to de-emphasise weight loss as a health goal and reduce stigma towards people who live in larger bodies. It promotes weight inclusivity, eating for wellbeing, respectful care, life-enhancing movement and health enhancement.

INTUITIVE EATING: Intuitive Eating is an evidence-based, weight-neutral, mind-body health approach, comprised of 10 principles and created by two dietitians, Evelyn Tribole and Elyse Resch in 1995. Intuitive Eating is a personal process of honoring health by listening and responding to the direct messages of the body in order to meet your physical and psychological needs.

MINDFULNESS: The art and practice of being continuously present with our experience in a non-judgemental way.

BODY LOVE RESOURCES

More Than a Body: Your Body Is an Instrument, Not an Ornament, *by Lindsay Kite and Lexie Kite*

Body Positive Power: How Learning to Love Yourself will Save Your Life, *by Megan Jayne Crabbe aka @bodiposipanda*

What We Don't Talk About When We Talk About Fat, *by Aubrey Gordon*

The Body Is Not an Apology: The Power of Radical Self-Love, *by Sonya Renee Taylor*

Things No One Will Tell Fat Girls: A Handbook for Unapologetic Living, *by Jes Baker*

Body Kindness: Transform Your Life from the Inside Out – and Never Say Diet Again, *by Rebecca Scritchfield*

Big & Bold: Yoga for the Plus-Size Woman, by *Laura Burns*

Beyond Beautiful: A Practical Guide to Being Happy, Confident, and You in a Looks-Obsessed World, *by Anuschka Rees*

Embody: Learning to Love Your Unique Body (And Quiet That Critical Voice), *by Connie Sobczak*

INTUITIVE EATING RESOURCES

Anti-Diet: Reclaim Your Time, Money, Well-Being and Happiness Through Intuitive Eating, *by Christy Harrison*

Intuitive Eating: A Revolutionary Program That Works, *by Evelyn Tribole and Elyse Resch*

Just Eat It: How Intuitive Eating Can Help You Get Your Shit Together Around Food, *by Laura Thomas*

Eat Up: Food, Appetite and Eating What You Want, *by Ruby Tandoh*

The F*** It Diet: Eating Should Be Easy, *by Caroline Dooner*

The Wellness Rebel, *by Pixie Turner*

MINDFULNESS & SELF-COMPASSION RESOURCES

Self-Compassion: The Proven Power of being Kind to Yourself, *by Kristin Neff*

Radical Acceptance: Embracing Your Life with the Heart of a Buddha, *by Tara Brach*

Full Catastrophe Living: Using the Wisdom of Your Body and Mind to Face Stress, Pain, and Illness, *by Jon Kabat-Zinn*

Mindfulness for Women: Declutter Your Mind, Simplify Your Life, Find Time to Be, *by Vidyamala Birch*

PODCASTS

Body Kindness®, Transform Your Health and Never Say Diet -Rebecca Scritchfield

Maintenance Phase - Aubrey Gordon & Michael Hobbes

Food Psych - Christy Harrison

Love, Food - Julie Duffy Dillon

Body Image Podcast - Corinne Dobbas

Made Of Human - Sofie Hagen

GRATITUDES

Warmest heartfelt thanks to the Get It Done team, Alex Franzen, Lindsey Smith, Woz Flint, Lucy Giller, Kayla Floyd and Tracie Kendziora, without whom this tiny book would never have "got done".

Thank you Candace for invaluable feedback and friendship – you da best, girl– and Sean at Ubuntu Editorials for his smashin' suggestions. I seem to have had the best of South Africa for my editorial team, and they made sure the magic was as potent as it could be. Love you guys!

Thanks, hand on heart, to the best gang of land mermaids a woman could wish for: Ula, Candy, Agata, Katy, Lois, Laverne, Caroline, Yvonne, the amazing Ursa Luna women, Geraldine, Audrey, Abbi, Rose, Charlotte, Marion, Theresa O., Suzanne, Sarah M, Mareike, Izzie, Kim, to name but a few!

Thank you to my biz buddies Candy, Theresa S., Clio, Alison, Erin, the Keystone gang, and Michelle Ward - biz-midwife extraordinaire. This is the best time to be a shepreneur!

Thank you to Karen, mindfulness mentor and ever-supportive friend.

Thank you to Catherine, who writes amazing books about exceptional women. You have been an inspiration since childhood.

Thank you to the intuitive eating and body image healing goddesses: Christy Harrison, Evelyn Tribole, Elyse Resch, Lindsay and Lexie Kite, Laura Thomas, Caroline Dooner, Rebecca Scritchfield, Geneen Roth, Audrey and Sophie Boss, Marci Evans, Fiona Sutherland, Megan Jayne Crabbe, Jes Baker, Virgie Tovar, Aubrey Gordon, Rachel Cole, Ruby Tandoh, Isobel Foxen-Duke, Pixie Turner, Sofie Hagen, Jameela Jamil, Ragen Chastain, and so many more.

The hugest thanks to my clients and all the women who have let me hold space for their body story so far.

Thank you to all my family; to the pea, who makes me laugh so hard it hurts (in a good way); and to my nieces - may they keep their body image mermaid powers forever close to heart.

Finally, thank you to you, dear reader. If one of my spells made you feel less alone and that bit more self-accepting, my job is done.

D ri Marie is an intuitive eating coach and body image healer. Clients praise her for her highly compassionate, fun, transformative and deeply intuitive sessions and for her wise, kind, funny and empathic personality.

A former actress, she is best known for having played Suzette on TV series "*Outlander*" - a maid with zero body image issues - and innumerable theatre parts, including a bar of chocolate.

She lives in Edinburgh with her crazy-but-oh-so-cute cat Wasabi and one of her besties. She is nourished by quality time with family and friends, nature, reading, creativity of all kinds, comic books, fairy tales, delish seasonal foods, retreats, exceedingly weird herbal teas and silly playfulness.

Body Love Magic is her first book.

CPSIA information can be obtained
at www.ICGtesting.com
Printed in the USA
BVHW040953011121
620445BV00015B/641